Contents

Chapter 1
Trouble with
Mr Grimstock

"Come on, Duke! Time for work!" called
Hattie.

Duke leaped off his bed and bounded
into the tiny hall. He wagged his huge
tail happily. Hattie was a lifeguard and
Duke loved helping her.

"Watch out!" laughed Hattie. "You'll
knock me over!"

Hattie was small. Duke was big –
very big! It was a good thing too,
because Duke was a lifeguard dog.
He was a special sort of dog called a
Newfoundland. He had two layers of fur:
one to keep him warm and one to keep
the water off. He also had webbed paws,
which helped him to swim.

7

He helped Hattie in her job as a lifeguard. They patrolled the beaches together. He could swim out to help people, then he would haul them back to shore. He had saved lots of children.

Hattie did up Duke's special red and yellow jacket, then they set out from their little cottage, down the path to the beach. It was a lovely summer morning and Duke ran ahead. He was free to play while Hattie checked the weather station and the flags.

"Mum, there's Duke!" called a little boy. "Can I go and play with him?"

His mum was setting up a windbreak. "Of course you can, Tim!" she smiled. Duke made everyone smile.

Tim grabbed a tennis ball and threw it into the sea. *Splash!* Duke flung himself into the water and grabbed the ball.

Then Duke swam back. He stood on the sand and shook himself. This was the moment Tim loved. Duke made his own rainstorm! Tim laughed with delight as the huge droplets showered him. Duke dropped the ball on the sand and Tim threw it again. They played and played until they heard Hattie's whistle.

At once, Duke stopped and cocked his head to one side. "I'm sorry," he seemed to say. "I have to go now." And he ran over to join Hattie.

Hattie and Duke took a long walk around the entire beach. Every day Hattie had to make sure that everything was safe. By the time they had finished, the beach was busy. There were lots of people in swimsuits and shorts. But one man was wearing a suit and carrying a briefcase. He looked very out of place.

"I wonder who that can be?" said Hattie to Duke. "Do you think he's looking for us? I hope nothing terrible has happened!"

Sure enough, the man started striding towards them.

Duke barked excitedly. He liked meeting new people. But this man didn't look at all friendly.

"Harriet Hammond?" said the man.
"I was told you'd be here."

Duke didn't growl but he showed his
teeth. He didn't like the way this man
was speaking to Hattie.

"Yes, I'm Harriet Hammond," said
Hattie. She put her hand on Duke's head.
"But most people call me Hattie. Can I
help you? I hope nothing is wrong?"

"There certainly is something wrong!" snapped the man. "There are no dogs allowed on this beach!"

Hattie's jaw dropped. "But Duke is a lifeguard dog!" she said. "He has rescued lots of children!"

"We have *people* to do that!" said the man. "And *lifeboats*! We don't need dogs!"

Hattie cleared her throat. "I'm sorry, Mr …? I don't know your name."

"Grimstock," said the man. "I'm the new Head of Tourism."

"Ah, I see," said Hattie. "I thought you must be new around here. Everyone knows about Duke. He's no ordinary dog. He never makes a mess on the beach and he has a very important job."

"A dog is a dog," said Mr Grimstock. "And no dogs are allowed on this beach. Especially very big ones! Take him home at once. If you don't, you'll have to pay a very large fine!"

"What?" gasped Hattie. "But I can't go home! I have to do my job! I can't leave Duke in the cottage all day! He'll howl! And anyway, he's a lifeguard!"

"He is *not* a lifeguard, he is a dog!" said Mr Grimstock. "Take him home right now, or you'll be sorry!"

Hattie's ordinarily cheerful face

flushed but she didn't say anything.
Duke rubbed his head against her hip
and whined. He didn't like the way her
mouth looked – all thin and tight as if
she had tasted something nasty.

Hattie turned away quickly and
marched off towards the cottage. Duke
followed with his tail between his legs.

Chapter 2
A Meeting at Georgio's

Back home, Duke flopped down in his basket. He buried his nose in his paws.

But Hattie was not the sort of person to mope. "Cheer up, Duke!" she said. "We'll soon sort this out."

She got out her favourite spotty teapot and brewed a big pot of tea. Then she cut a thick wedge of fruit cake and sat down to make a plan.

She made a lot of phone calls and sent loads of emails. Duke was so bored that he fell asleep.

He didn't wake up until Hattie said, "Come on, Duke! We're going to Georgio's!"

Duke loved Georgio's, the local fish and chip shop. Georgio could always find some treats for Duke – half a fishcake or a few chips or, if he was really lucky, some scampi. Thinking about scampi made Duke drool.

Duke bounded down the lane after
Hattie. Georgio had won 'Best in the
West Chip Shop' for three years running.
There was always a queue outside. But
it had never been as busy as this! Duke
couldn't even see the shop, there were
so many people crammed in front of it.
They were sitting on the chairs and the
low wall and some were standing. The
odd thing was, Duke knew them all!

All the other lifeguards were there, and so was the crew of the lifeboat. Bob from the beach shop was talking to Izzy from the ice cream parlour. Dot, who ran the general store, was chatting to Mr Walker, the head teacher from the village school. And there were simply loads of children!

"What is going on? Will there be any chips left for me?" Duke wondered.

"Here they are!" shouted Tim and he came running up to meet them. "Come on, Duke! Come on, Hattie! We're all waiting!"

"Waiting?" thought Duke. "What for?" Whatever it was, it seemed very exciting – so exciting that he nuzzled up really close to Tim.

"You need to be on your best
behaviour, Duke," said Hattie. "All these
people are here because of you!"

"Because of me?" thought Duke. Lots
of children were running up to stroke
him but Hattie clipped on Duke's lead
and led him on to the terrace.

Chapter 3
No Stopping Duke!

"Sit, Duke!" said Hattie, and then she climbed on to one of the tables!

"Thank you so much for coming, everyone," she said, in her loudest voice. "As you know, Duke has been told he can't be a lifeguard dog any more. Mr Grimstock, the new Head of Tourism, won't allow it."

"Why not?" asked Tim's sister, Poppy.

"Some people don't like dogs on beaches," explained Tim. "They might scare little children and eat people's picnics."

Duke was upset. He never scared anyone or ate their picnics! He barked loudly.

"Sssh, Duke, it's OK," said Hattie. "All these people are here to help."

"We should have a petition," called out Bob.

"What's that?" asked Poppy.

"It's a list of names of all the people who think Duke should still be a lifeguard," said Tim.

"Yes, we must have a petition," said Hattie. "So I've made a form and I hope you will all sign it this afternoon."

"Hear hear!" shouted Jack, the lifeboat captain.

"We should have a protest," called out Izzy. "We can march to the council offices with banners."

"We could take our dogs too," said someone else.

"The children can write letters at school," said Mr Walker, the head teacher.

"And we could make posters!" called out a girl from year 6.

"We could have a charity dog show!" said Dot. "For the lifeboat fund. That'll show this Mr Grimstock how useful dogs can be!"

Hattie beamed. "Those are all great ideas," she said. "Thank you so much. And, of course, we can all write to Mr Grimstock or phone him. I've started a web page so we can all keep in touch. I'm sure it won't be long before Duke is back to work!"

"Hear hear!" shouted Bob, and everyone joined in.

Hattie held up her hand for quiet. "And now," she said, smiling around at everybody, "let's get signing!"

"Just a minute!"

Everyone turned to look at the thin young man who had stepped forward.

"Yes?" said Hattie. "Do I know you?"

"Not yet," said the young man. "I'm Brent Brown from the *Western Gazette*. I'm here to report on this story."

"Really?" said Hattie, eagerly. "That will be wonderful! We'd be so grateful for your help!"

Brent Brown cleared his throat and looked uncomfortable. "I'm not so sure about that," he said.

Hattie looked puzzled and there were some angry mutters from the crowd.

"But why not?" asked Hattie.

"Because lots of people want to keep dogs off beaches. We receive hundreds of emails at the *Gazette* that say so."

"I don't think you understand, Mr Brown," said Hattie. "Duke is not just any old dog – Duke is a lifeguard dog."

"A dog is a dog," said Brent Brown. He shrugged his shoulders. "I'm sorry. Now, can I ask a few questions, please?"

Georgio pushed his way to the front of the crowd. "A dog is a dog, is it, Mr Brown?" he said. "Well, a customer is a customer! But I don't want a customer like you! So get off my terrace, please. Everyone else – this way for free chips!"

Then he bent down and ruffled Duke's fur. "Good dog, Duke," he said. "You wait here and I'll bring you a treat! How about some scampi?" Georgio led everyone into the chip shop – everyone except Brent Brown.

Brent Brown glared after them. Then he got out his phone.

Chapter 4
Things Get Worse
For Hattie

The next day, Duke woke with a start.
Hattie's phone was ringing. She reached
out from under her duvet and peered at
the screen.

"It's only half past six!" Hattie
mumbled. She gasped. "Oh no, it's Jack!"

Jack was the lifeboat captain. Duke
jumped up. That might mean the lifeboat
was being launched. But it didn't sound
like it.

"Yes, I agree," Hattie was saying to Jack. "We can't let this stop us. We must just carry on. Yes, thanks for letting me know."

Hattie put down the phone and sighed. "Oh dear, Duke," she said. "That reporter Brent Brown has written a nasty article about us in the *Western Gazette*. I must have upset him – or maybe Georgio did. I'd better look on the *Gazette*'s website."

Hattie pulled a big sweater over her pyjamas and ran down the stairs. Duke bounded after her. She put the kettle on and then sat down at her laptop. Moments later, she leaned back, looking upset.

"Oh dear, this is awful!" she cried.

Duke padded over and rested his head on Hattie's lap.

"Look, Duke!" she said. "There's a photo of you barking! It makes you look horrible. And listen to what he's written!" She read the web page out loud.

Dirty Dog Drama!

The peace of a pretty seaside village was ruined last night when Harriet Hammond, a local lifeguard, made a scene outside Georgio's fish and chip shop. Standing on a table, she persuaded local people that her huge pet dog is a lifeguard dog and should be allowed on the beach. Of course, there is no such thing as a lifeguard dog. The chip shop manager then gave free chips to all Miss Hammond's supporters.

Hattie put her head in her hands. "It's not fair," she said. "He's made us sound dreadful!"

Duke whined and put his big paw on her knee. He hated to see Hattie so sad.

She stroked his head. "Oh Duke," she said. "I can't let this get me down. We just have to carry on, don't we?"

Duke nuzzled Hattie's face. Then he grabbed the cuff of her sleeve and tugged. He knew they'd both feel better if they went for a walk.

Chapter 5
Everyone Helps Out

Everyone who came to the meeting at
Georgio's did exactly what they said
they would do. Soon every shop in the
village was plastered with the children's
posters and drawings of Duke. All the
junior school children wrote letters to
Mr Grimstock and the infants drew
pictures of Duke rescuing people.

Brent Brown wrote in the *Gazette* that
Mr Walker, the head teacher, was not
doing his job properly. He should make
the children stick to *important* subjects
like maths and science and spelling.

Dot's dog show was a delight. Every
sort of dog was there, from tiny terriers
to huge hounds. The highlight was the
talent show. There was a spaniel that
joined in when his owner played the
recorder. There was a Jack Russell terrier
that could jump through hoops and play
dead. Best of all, there was a Labrador
that could collect up the dirty laundry
for his owner, who used a wheelchair.

"Mr Grimstock should see how clever these dogs are!" said Dot. "Then he might believe there's such a thing as a lifeguard dog!"

"I do hope so," said Hattie. "Thank you so much."

Brent Brown wrote that people who lived near the village hall had complained about the terrible noise. But he did print a photo of the Labrador gathering up the laundry.

Izzy organized a special dog walk to the council offices. She led the way with her Yorkshire terrier, Sweetie. Duke and Hattie brought up the rear. All sorts of dogs joined in. No one seemed to mind that other dogs were banned from the beach – but everyone minded about Duke.

"He saved my Rickie's life," said a lady with a bulldog. "He'd got out of his depth. Duke got to him before anyone else had noticed!"

"That's right," said a man with a German shepherd dog. "He swam out and rescued a surfer caught in a current – no one else was strong enough."

When they got to the council offices, they waved their banners and chanted slogans.

But nothing happened. They shouted louder.

Hattie went to speak to the lady at
the front desk. "Could Mr Grimstock
come out and speak to us, please?"

But the lady at the front desk said
that Mr Grimstock was far too busy in
a very important meeting about cleaner
coastlines. He could not be disturbed.

"What? All day?" said Hattie.

"Yes, *all day*," said the lady at the front desk.

Everyone was very tired and fed up. Then Georgio arrived with his mobile chip van. They all cheered.

Brent Brown wrote that it was disappointing that Mr Grimstock had not come out to meet the crowd and that all the dogs and children had been very well behaved. He printed a picture of everyone looking very hot and tired.

Chapter 6
It's Hopeless!

After the special dog walk, Hattie had a meeting with Jack, Izzy, Dot, Georgio and Mr Walker.

"It's no good," she said. "Mr Grimstock isn't going to change his mind. And I can't leave Duke alone in the cottage all day. I'm just going to have to give up my job. I can't do it with him and I can't do it without him."

"No!" said Jack. He thumped the table with his fist. "You and Duke are the best lifeguards we've got!"

"I just don't see what else I can do!" said Hattie. "I'm so sorry."

Sadly, her friends went home. They had run out of ideas. Hattie sat down at her laptop and wrote an email to the coastguard. Then she curled up on the sofa and began to cry. Duke jumped up beside her and nuzzled her.

She wrapped her arms around him
and buried her face in his fur. Duke
knew there was something badly wrong.
He was never allowed on the sofa but
this time Hattie didn't push him off. She
cried until she fell asleep with her arms
around Duke's neck.

Boom! A huge crash of thunder! The
room lit up and then there was another
huge boom. Duke sprang off the sofa and
Hattie staggered to her feet.

"Goodness, listen to that rain!" she said.

It sounded as if pebbles were
pounding the windows. The wind
howled around the cottage.

"Brr! It's gone so cold!" said Hattie
and she hurried to draw the curtains.
But then she stopped.

"Oh no!" Hattie cried. "They're
trying to launch the lifeboat! Someone
must be out there! Come on, Duke – it's
so windy, they might need some help!"

Chapter 7
Duke to the Rescue!

Hattie pulled on her waterproof coat.
She fastened Duke into his jacket. Then
she grabbed a torch. They hurried down
the path that led to the beach. Hattie
had to hang on to Duke's collar to stop
herself from being blown over. Sand blew
up in their faces and stung their eyes.

The lifeboat crew was having no
luck getting the boat launched. The
waves were so big that it kept being
forced back.

"Can we help?" Hattie yelled at Jack.

"I don't know!" Jack shouted back.
"There's a dinghy out there and a
teenage boy's overboard. We just
can't get to him."

Duke whined and pawed at
Hattie. "No, Duke," she said. "It's too
dangerous."

But Duke whined again and ran
towards the crashing waves.

"Hattie, Duke might be our only
chance," shouted Jack. "We've tried and
tried to get the boat launched. The boy's
parents are frantic."

Hattie glanced over to where a couple
was standing, their arms around each
other, staring out into the storm. She
gulped. "All right," she yelled. "Give me
a line and a lifebelt."

Working as fast as she could, Hattie
strapped an extra float on to Duke.
Then she fastened a strong line and a
lifebelt to his jacket.

"Right, everyone," she shouted.
"Hold this line! If we lose it, we lose
the boy and Duke as well! Wrap it
around your waists!"

The lifeboat crew grasped the line
with Hattie.

"You too!" shouted Jack at the boy's
parents. "You can help!"

Hattie gave Duke the word. He
plunged into the crashing waves.

Everyone dug their heels into the sand
and held on, as hard as they could. It was
very dark. There was so much spray that
they soon lost sight of Duke. But they
could tell he was swimming away because
more and more of the line was vanishing
into the sea.

Suddenly, it went slack.

Hattie gulped. She felt sick. "Duke!"
she whispered. "Duke! Please be all right!"

Nothing happened. Then the line
felt heavier. It seemed tighter. "Am I
imagining it?" wondered Hattie. No, Jack
was yelling at them to pull.

"I think Duke's got the boy!" he shouted. "Pull, everyone, pull! Together! Now!"

They all leaned back and heaved so hard that they nearly fell over. They couldn't see a thing but they kept on pulling.

"Come on, Duke!" Hattie yelled. "Come on! Here, Duke here!"

She pulled until she thought she couldn't pull any more.

Then suddenly, there was
Duke, scrabbling in the sand. He
was dragging a boy in a lifebelt. Was
the boy alive? They all ran forward.

"It's OK!" shouted Hattie. "He's
breathing!" And at that moment,
the ambulance arrived, its blue lights
flashing.

Then Hattie turned to Duke, who was lying on the sand, panting. She threw her arms around him. "Duke!" she cried. "Brave, brave Duke! How can anyone say you're not a lifeguard?"

Duke staggered to his feet and nuzzled her hand feebly. The worst of the storm was over but the wind was still strong. It blew them back up the beach towards the ambulance. The boy was on a stretcher, and his mum was holding his hand. His dad was waiting by the ambulance steps.

Hattie stopped and stared at the boy's dad. Surely she must be dreaming? Surely it couldn't be – Mr Grimstock?

But it was! His face was white. He
held out his hand. Silently, Hattie took
it in hers.

"Forgive me," said Mr Grimstock, in
a voice which shook. "I was wrong. How
can I thank you enough?"

"It's Duke you need to thank, not
me," said Hattie.

Mr Grimstock patted Duke's big
head. "Thank you so much, Duke," he
said. "I am so sorry. There *is* such a
thing as a lifeguard dog and you are
the best one in the world! I am going to
make sure you get a medal for bravery."

Hattie smiled. "I'm sure he'd rather
have some scampi and chips," she said.
"As a very special treat!"

"Then he shall have those too!" said
Mr Grimstock.

The next week, there was a huge photo of Duke on the front page of the *Western Gazette*. Brent Brown had written an exciting account of his daring rescue. 'A dog is not always just a dog,' he wrote. 'Sometimes a dog is a hero.' And at the top, he put the headline: 'Duke, the Lifeguard Dog – Our Local Hero!'

About the author

I keep a scrapbook of story ideas. I find snippets from newspapers and websites – sometimes pictures, sometimes stories. Then, maybe years later, the story grows from the snippet. This story was one of those. A long time ago, I read about a real, live lifeguard dog and the story grew from there.

And I once had a dog. He was the most loveable dog you ever met. He wasn't a Newfoundland but a springer spaniel. But when my Lifeguard Dog grabs Hannah's sleeve and tugs her out for a walk, that's just like my Duke!